THE
Archive Photographs
SERIES

PENISTONE

Thirtieth Annual
SUNDAY SCHOOL EXCURSION.

The Committee of the Penistone, Thurlstone, and Bullhouse Sunday
Schools beg to announce that they have made arrangements
with the G. C. Ry. Co., for a Day Trip to

LLANDUDNO

ON

Wednesday, June 28th, 1899

The Train will leave

WORTLEY at 4-0 a.m.
PENISTONE 4-15 „
HAZLEHEAD 4-25 „
DUNFORD 4-30 „

Fare for Double Journey,
ONE DAY,

4s.

Children under 12 years of age half the above fares.

Returning from Llandudno at 7.30 p.m.

Special Tickets may be obtained extending the stay to 2, 3 or 4 days for 6/6
each, 5 or 6 days 8/- each.

Passengers holding long-period Tickets at higher fares return from Llandudno
by any ordinary train (Mail and Boat Expresses excepted) *via* Manchester, on the
dates specified.

Tickets may be obtained on the Morning of the Trip at
Penistone Station only.

TICKETS may be obtained from the following persons :— PENISTONE, Jno. Jagger, Tom Taylor, Hy. Gilpin,
Frank Tinker, H. Jordan ; THURLSTONE, J. W. Snaa, Chas. Kay, Oliver Smith, Geo. Beard, Arthur
Whiteley, Tom Crossland, John Watts ; BULLHOUS, Walter Bramall ; LANGSETT, Herbert Watts ;
CROWEDGE, Smith Howard ; HOYLANDSWAINE, Jno. Cleland.

James H. Wood, The "Don" ress, Penistone.

A Sunday School outing to Llandudno in 1899.

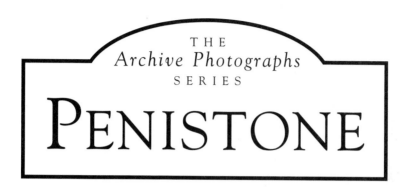

THE
Archive Photographs
SERIES

PENISTONE

Compiled by
David Hambleton and Matthew Young

CHALFORD

First published 1995
Copyright © David Hambleton and Matthew Young, 1995

The Chalford Publishing Company Ltd
St Mary's Mill
Chalford
Stroud
Gloucestershire GL6 8NX

ISBN 0 7524 00138 6

Typesetting and origination by
The Chalford Publishing Company Ltd
Printed in Great Britain by
Redwood Books, Trowbridge

Entertainers from Netherfield Cricket Club in the 1920s.

Contents

Acknowledgements

Many thanks must go to those who provided photographs and information including Joan Crossland, Margaret Marsh, Margaret Beard, Gladys Turner, Jack Jubb, Malcolm Hambleton, Eric Crossley and B arbara Marshall.

Any factual errors or mistakes are entirely the responsibility of the authors but we would appreciate any further information on the pictures shown here.

This book is dedicated to Maureen Hambleton – in loving memory.

Thurlstone Band, 28 June 1952.

Introduction

The pictures in this collection, many previously unpublished, date from the turn of the century to recent times and chart the transformation that Penistone has undergone. The book is a progression through the rise and decline of the steel industry; creeping urbanisation and the expansion of the rail network. A century's change may be sweeping but the camera illuminates the detail and captures in an instant the very essence of time and place: the clothes, the homes, the faces. Penistone people at work, play and worship are frozen by the camera demonstrating a lifestyle that although slower was a constant struggle. As a well-known local historian said of Penistone folk: 'A life of toil has been the lot of these men from generation to generation, and the circumstances surrounding them have produced a race sturdy and massive as the square-built tower of their ancient church'.

From such hardy circumstances the town has produced men and women of note: the Wordsworth family from whom later generations produced the famous poet and a reforming bishop; Nicholas Saunderson, the seventeenth-century professor of mathematics at Cambridge, who legend states taught himself to read by feeling the letters upon the gravestones; and Heather Armitage, the local schoolgirl who ran for England. Public buildings and institutions have been created for the benefit of all: the Grammar School, founded in 1392, is one of the oldest educational establishments in the country; the Town Hall and Assembly Rooms provide for civic occasions. A gritty determination to succeed coupled with a fine sense of humour is undoubtedly a Penistone trait – a precedent set by the founders of the town.

Today Penistone is a bustling market town and the centre of commerce and social activity for many smaller villages and hamlets – each with its own sense of community. There have been many changes to the area: buildings have been removed, new shops have emerged and an influx of a new population to the area who make their living in Huddersfield, Sheffield, or Barnsley. However, even a recent visitor to the town will recognise some of the streets and buildings shown here; older residents will be familiar with many of the names, faces and clubs. These pictures are a thread to our past and demonstrate that Penistone has a flourishing community that remains resolutely independent – long may it continue.

> *O give me but some Yorkshire fare,*
> *A Yorkshire scene, some Yorkshire air,*
> *Where lads are bold and lasses fair and*
> *I'm contented.*
>
> W. Danby

David Hambleton and Matthew Young
February, 1995

Not quite Wimbledon! A tennis match at Penistone in the 1920s; the clothes obviously designed for a sleek and rapid game.

One

Penistone

Market Street *c.* 1910. A market had been held in the area since the thirteenth century but the charter for Penistone was not granted until 1698.

Another view of Market Street. Beside the carriage on the left is R.D. Woodcocks: a superstore of its time, Woodcocks sold hardware and furniture. The founder, Risdon Darracott Woodcock, was originally a cobbler and the store also sold a variety of boots and shoes. As Mr Woodcock's daughter Nellie stated: 'As people in the area asked for various goods my father agreed to provide them until the stock grew and grew and there was scarcely anything we didn't sell.'

High Street, *c.* 1900. The shops on the right were removed to make way for a supermarket. The gentleman peering out from the doorway is Mr Steven Washington.

The corner of St. Mary's Street and Market Street, *c.* 1900. Hudson and Birks, a footwear shop of note, was demolished in 1930 to make way for the National Provincial Bank. The National Provincial became the National Westminster in 1971.

Hunters Tea Stores staff, *c.* 1910

St. Mary's Street, *c.* 1935

Beast Market in 1894. The market was held in the streets until 1910 despite regulations from the Board of Agriculture and Fisheries of 1903 deeming that livestock be procured from enclosed surroundings. Eventually, as much due to health and sanitary reasons, room was made for the market at 'Backfields'.

St Mary's Street, c. 1910. The mound on the right is now occupied by the British Legion.

Biltcliffe's shop on Bridge Street. This famous photographic shop was started by Joshua Biltcliffe and also sold gramophones, violin strings, hosiery and the local school uniform. It was Biltcliffe's that created much of the photographic record of Penistone.

Joshua Biltcliffe, the founder of the Bridge Street Shop, was also a leading light in the local Netherfield choir.

The Penistone Co-operative Shop, c. 1900. The Co-operative belonged to the Barnsley branch. This building, affectionately known as 'the shack', was bought by the Penistone Theatre Group in the 1950s.

Bridge End, c. 1910. Most of the properties seen here were owned by John Taylor, the local Blacksmith, whose own business premises are by the horse and cart. The business was called 'Fred Taylor's' and as well as shoeing horses also manufactured pieces for David Brown Ltd. John Taylor was known locally by a nickname which, if uttered, was guaranteed to send iron implements airborne. There had been a blacksmiths on the site for over 300 years and at its peak employed three men shoeing eighty horses a week – the cost to shoe one horse was 5s 6d.

The edge of High Street and Market Street, *c*. 1900. The railings have been removed and the premises now belong to G.T. Newsagents.

High Street, *c.* 1890.

Willow House, Penistone, *c.* 1900. This residence belonged to Dr Arthur Wilson (born 1852), a local councillor and Medical Officer to Thurlstone and Penistone districts. His father, George, was Chairman of the Manchester Anti-Corn Law League. The house has now been divided into flats.

'The Grove', Green Road in 1909 was originally built in 1707 from two older cottages and was extended in 1830. It once belonged to Sammy Marsh and later to the Rolling family.

Church Street, c. 1905. The back of this postcard reads, tongue in cheek, that the receiver, Miss E Bailey, 'may be familiar with this view.'

Church Hill in 1908. On the far left is the ground now occupied by the Town Hall.

The Carnegie Free Library and the Town Hall. The library was built with donations from Andrew Carnegie and was opened by the Earl of Wharncliffe in 1913. A year later the hall and committee rooms were opened. The hall is now part of Metro Cinemas.

A view of Water Hall, c. 1930. The hall was the old family home of the Wordsworth family. Descendants of the Water Hall family later became Bishop of Lincoln and a rather famous poet. The land around the hall is now occupied by new estates.

Water Hall Bridge over the River Don.

Netherfield Villas which are directly opposite the Grammar School.

Cubley Hall, *c.* 1930s. The hall was for many years a Childrens Home but has recently been converted to a bar and restaurant.

Scout Dam at the back of the Grammar School, *c.* 1920. The bridge has since been removed.

A picture taken from Scout Bridge in 1910. The Reservoir Filter House, which was constructed in the late 1920s, now resides in the upper fields.

Two

People and Processions

Inside the British Legion and Ex-Servicemen's Club.

The Duke of Windsor visited Penistone on 15 December 1933 and inspected the Occupational Centre that had opened to help workers made redundant by the closure of the Cammell Laird Works three years earlier. The Duke was to abdicate just three years later after his notorious liaison with Mrs Simpson.

The funeral of Mr J Matherson, a Crimean War Veteran, 31 January 1915.

European War Volunteers (Penistone), part of the Sheffield Battalion of the Yorkshire and Lancaster Regiment, *c.* 1914.

European War Volunteers on Penistone Station. The enthusiasm for volunteering at the outbreak of the Great War was often evident in pictoral records – the sickening horrors to come unbeknown to the smiling faces.

Penistone War Memorial unveiled in August 1924.

Medical Volunteers for the Second World War, *c.* 1940s.

Medical Volunteers go through their drill, *c.* 1940s

Penistone Boys Brigade outside Netherfield Chapel, *c*. 1950.

Market Street during the Parade of 1919.

The Peace Parade. Many such processions took place to celebrate the end of four years of a horrific war.

A Whitsuntide Walk in the 1920s. The Whit Walks date back over one hundred years and were a celebration under the auspices of the Sheffield Sunday School Union.

A Walk passes Thurlstone Post Office.

Penistone Feast Monday 1926.

Penistone Wesleyans outside the chapel in 1925. The Reverand Langton can be seen in the left doorway.

Penistone Agricultural Sho, 1906. The show was one hundred years old in 1972 although a gathering had been held alternately between Wortley and Penistone since the beginning of the nineteenth century. In 1883 the show was moved from Thursday to Saturday to avoid Market Day and in 1906 it attracted 1,623 visitors which rose to over 15,000 in 1926.

Penistone Show 1914. The show was discontinued during the war years.

Millhouse Show 1909.

Men's Effort *c.* 1910 at the back of Willow House. Back row, left to right: G.J. Hinchcliff, J. Davis, T. Pinder, F. Hinchcliff, J. Hinchcliff, C. Rayner, J. Dickenson, T. Hanson, F. Creswick, H. Whitehead, T. Brearley. Front row: R. Taylor, W. Taylor, J. Bonner, R. Wood, W. Wadsworth.

Ladies dressed for Whitsuntide. The only identified member of the group is Nellie Whitehead.

Chris Fallas, for many years the gravedigger at Penistone, owned this donkey and cart. The boy pictured is thought to Gordon Bashforth.

Washing Day at Vernon Terrace, *c.* 1910.

Mrs Gertrude Penney outside her house in Don Street, Spring Vale, *c*. 1920s.

James 'Pot Oil' Ashton, the Penistone Town Crier *c*. 1920. Ashton was well known throughout Penistone and achieved notoriety after leaving his bell one night at a local Public House and disappearing forever.

Jubilee Bonfire, c. 1920s

A snowhouse built for the children of Penistone at the turn of the century.

A picnic at Gravels Farm, 1 August 1910.

Thurlstone and Millhouse Musical Society Picnic at Parkin House, 1910.

Spring Vale Methodist Chapel Sunday School, *c.* 1950.

Wesleyan Sunday School and teachers in 1912.

PENISTONE ST. PAUL'S W.D.H.
1st PRIZE WINNERS, SOUTH YORKSHIRE MUSICAL FESTIVAL
FEMALE VOICE CHOIRS, 1935.

Miss Mona Burkinshaw (cup holder) was a prime mover in the Operatic Society and the conductor for the St. Pauls Female Choir which won first prize at the South Yorkshire Musical Festival in 1935.

The Operatic Society performing *Dogs of Devon* in 1922 at the Town Hall.

A happy audience for a concert at Penistone St. Paul's Methodist Chapel.

Thurlstone Primitive Methodist Sunday School, winners of the William Smith Shield. The Shield was named after the founder of the Sunday School at Penistone and was awarded annually for the best Sunday School.

51

THE MERRIUNS CONCERT PARTY

Thurlstone Primitive Methodists Chapel Concert Party 'the Merriuns (Merry Ones)', *c.* 1920s. Those identified so far are John Arthur Blacker, Jesse Blacker, Ada Blacker, George Tinker and Kathleen Booth.

Three of the Merriuns – George Redvers Tinker, John Arthur Blacker and Jim Windle.

Stone laying ceremony at the Primitive Chapel in Thurlstone, 25 April 1914.

Thurlstone Wesleyan Choir 1908.

A gathering in front of Thurlstone Wesleyan Chapel.

A 'boatfloat' during Jubilee Day 1935.

Netherfield Congregational Choir 1902. From the top, left to right: Mr C. Ellis, Miss Annie Smith, Mr Risdon Woodcock, Mr Joshua Biltcliffe, Miss Kate Winterbottom, Mr Thomas Fielding, Mr Tom Dyson, Miss L. Moorhouse, Miss L. Smith, Miss E. Fielding, Miss C. Nicholson, Miss S. Mitchell, Miss M. Wood, Miss Stewart, Mr H. Bates, Mr R. Goddard.

King George and Queen Mary's visit to Penistone on 11 July 1912; the couple passed through on a tour of the West Riding. The first 'official' visit was made by the Duke of Windsor in 1933.

The Royal Visit, 1912. As the King and Queen passed through seven hundred children who had gathered in the town centre sang the National Anthem.

Centenary Year for the Sunday School at Bullhouse Chapel, 1925.

Outside Ingbirchworth Chapel, *c.* 1910. The occasion is unknown.

An anniversary at Ingbirchworth Chapel, *c.* 1950s. The wall paintings have since been removed.

The wedding of Mrs Gertrude Penney at Springvale in the 1920s.

A gentlemen's gathering at the Old Vicarage Lawn, *c*. 1930s.

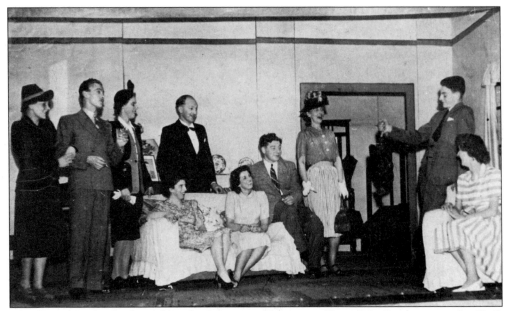

The first ever play performed by the Penistone Players was *Young Mrs Barrington* at the Drill Hall on 11 November 1948. The cast were J. Graham Kelsey, Joan Crossland, Esther Kelsey, Jesse Bottom, Beryl Duckett, Mary Hinchcliff, John G. Smith, Gordon W. Smith, Hanley Taylor, Kitty Taylor.

The Netherfield Pierrot Players in costume, 1920s.

A group outside the Old Tin Chapel. Back row, from left to right: Albert Singleton, Wilfred Scrivens, George Singleton, Norman Robinson, Harold Kaye. Front row: Thomas Steel, Arthur Bywaters, Cecil Penney, Oliver Penney, Owen Roebuck, John Robinson.

Harvest Thanksgiving at Springvale Methodist Church, 1948.

CODY'S AEROPLANE AT PENIST

Cody's aeroplane at Nethermill November 1909. The plane was passing through Penistone

IC NOV 4 1909

after being exhibited at the Doncaster Airshow; the show ran for two years (1909 and 1910).

Cutting the first sod at Scout Dyke Reservoir, 22 May 1924.

Peace Parade on Bridge Street in 1919.

Co-operative Jubilee on 18 July.

Nursing Association Parade in the 1920s.

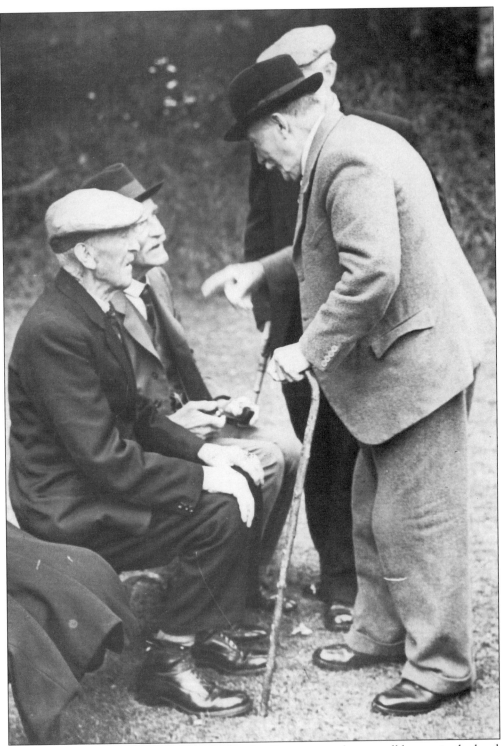

Peace Brothers, c. 1920s. The Peace twins lived in Penistone and were well known in the local area.

Three

The Villages

Looking across the moors toward the 'Flouch' Pub, *c*. 1920s.

Bullhouse Bridge in 1920.

Manchester Road, Thurlstone 1904.

Top of Town, Thurlstone 1905.

Top of Town, Thurlstone, c. 1900.

The Black Bull Hotel, Thurlstone, in the 1920s.

West Cliff, Thurlstone, 1905.

Tenter Hill, Thurlstone *c.* 1930s. The weavers' cottages shown demonstrate the three levels essential for a basic cottage industry: workplace, living area and storage.

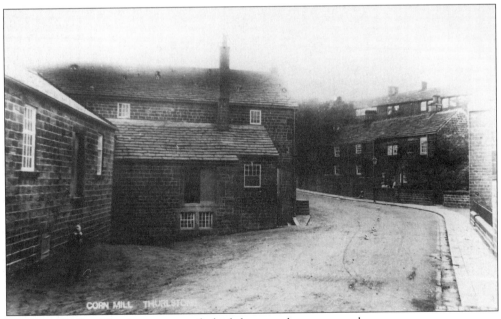

The Corn Mill at Thurlstone most of which has now been removed.

Prospect House, Thurlstone, 1904.

Summer Ford Bridge, 1940. The bridge was part of the old highway but is now only visible at the bottom of Ingbirchworth Reservoir during severe droughts.

Ingbirchworth Reservoir in the late 1920s. The filter system pictured here has since been rebuilt.

Cat Hill Farm. The house was designed by Dr Catlin in 1584 and was a half way stop for travellers between Wakefield and Manchester. At one time the Stanhopes, a renowned Yorkshire family, owned the property.

Wire Mill at Oxspring; originally a 'filling' mill which degreased wool it became a wire mill in 1888. The mill became operated by an engine in 1896 but the waterwheel was not removed until 1958.

Four Lane Ends at Oxspring *c.* 1900. The pub on the corner is the Travellers Inn.

Langsett Moors, *c.* 1920s.

CARLECOTES HALL

Carlecotes Hall was originally owned by Adam Eyre who achieved fame as a commander in the Parliamentary Army under Sir Thomas Fairfax. The Hall later came into the possession of Charles Chapman, the master of the Penistone Hunt from 1887 to 1894.

Ivy Bank, Ingbirchworth *c.* 1930. The house belongs to the Beever family.

Mustard Hill, Hoylandswaine, *c*. 1920.

A Shepherds Meeting at Saltersbrook in 1907. The Millers Arms is no longer standing.

Four

Sport and Leisure

Bridge Hotel Football Team at Bridge End, *c.* 1910.

Penistone Church Football Club – winners of the Sheffield Junior Cup 1936 and 1937.

Penistone Church Football Team, *c*. 1930.

Ladies Wesleyan Cricket Club, *c.* 1910.

Netherfield Cricket Club, *c.* 1910. The only identified member so far is George Winterbottom.

Netherfield CC in 1938. Those identified so far are: Ronnie Littlewood, Donald Marsh, Joe Wood, Stanley Palmer, Ned Mather, Norman Wood, Peter Broadhead, Reg Proud, Tommy Priest, Jack Burkinshaw, George Fowler, Colin Bashforth.

Netherfield CC during the 1930s. Those identified so far are: Jack Burkinshaw, James Marsh, Harold Marsh, Colin Radcliffe, Tommy Marsh, Tommy Priest, Frank Caffrey, Oliver Roebuck, George Holden, Peter Hinchcliff, Donald Marsh, Ned Mather.

Penistone Iron and Steel 2nd XI in the 1930s. Those identified so far are: Bill Vickerstaff, Brian Lee, George Fowler, Albert Kilner, John Chandler, Douglas Walsh, Frank Ellis, Gladstone Masheder, Gordon Bradley, Percy Crossland, Lionel Maud, John Smethhurst, Jack Mellor.

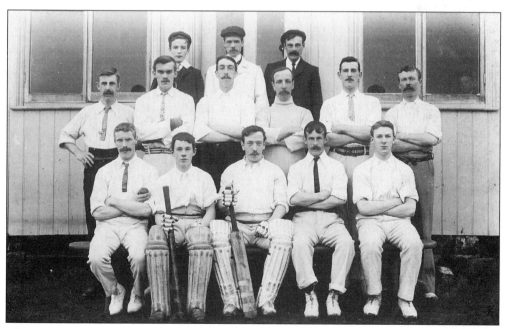

Thurlstone Wesleyan Cricket Club 1908 – that year's winners of the Penistone and District League.

Thurlstone Cricket Club 1907.

Penistone and Thurlstone Golf Club at the Royde Moor Links, 1907. The annual subscription was ten shillings.

ENISTONE AND THURLSTONE GOLF CLUB OPENING OF PAVILION SEP 7 1907

The clubhouse pavilion near the first tee. The course was opened on 7 September 1907 and the first president was John Hinchcliff. The course was closed in 1913 and is now covered by the reservoir.

The Tennis Club on the Old Vicarage Lawn, *c*. 1920s.

A tennis match involving Penistone Players, *c*. 1950.

The Works Brass Band, *c.* 1920.

Thurlstone Handbell Ringers were formed in 1855. The minutes of the Thurlstone School Board states that the bell ringers should always have a room in which to rehearse. In 1930 Thurlstone took first prize in the English Championship.

The Operatic Society performing *My Lady Mollie* in 1949. The performers are Jean Mitchell, Kathleen Taylor, Joy Mather, Shelia Duckett, Mary Mitchell, Audrey Cherry, Margaret Marsh, Joan Crossland.

The 'Arcadians' at the Town Hall in 1953.

Five

Transport and Industry

Scout Dyke just before the start of construction, *c.* 1920s. The area around Penistone is perfect for the construction of reservoirs and within easy reach of the major metropolitan areas.

Compacting (puddling) the clay at Scout Dyke, *c.* 1922; a slow and labourious task for workers many of whom were Irish navvies. The reservoir was built to supply Barnsley.

Tipping on a bank near Puddle Trench.

The concreting process, c. 1924.

Bywash construction for the overflow.

The completed reservoir with a new Valve Tower.

The flood at Penistone on 4 September 1951. Looking toward Netherfield the bungalows in the background belonged to Hinchcliff family.

THE DON PENISTONE

The Weir at Penistone was removed in the 1970s as it was deemed to aid flooding.

The viaduct at Oxspring on the Barnsley Line.

Penistone Station, *c*. 1910.

An old locomotive on the road across Royd Moor.

Opposite: Penistone Viaduct (containing 29 arches) was built in 1849. On 2 February 1916 the second and third arches collapsed and a L&Y Tank Engine plunged into the banking. The engine then had to be cut into pieces and removed as the site could not be reached by crane.

Viaduct Collapse 1916. Despite the evident destruction the viaduct was re-opened in August of the same year.

A waggon smash in July 1916 on Board Hill Moor killed three men instantly.

Hoylandswaine smash July 1st 1908.

Alf Chappell nailmaking at Hoylandswaine.
The practice had been carried on at
Hoylandswaine for many years.

The tyre mill at Penistone Steelworks.

The old Cammell Laird site was developed as a foundary by David Brown Company in 1935. After the war the foundry built high pressure steam turbines for the rapidly expanding power industry.

Cammell Laird and Co. Ltd *c.* 1920s. The steel works were founded in Penistone in 1863 and employed at peak 1,500 men. Under the control of the English Steel Corporation the complex was closed in 1930.

The great snows of 1933 covered Penistone Market Street.

During the snowstorm of February 1933 all roads into Penistone were blocked. Doctor Arthur Gordon Wilson of Thurlstone walked nine miles to tend to a patient marooned on the Manchester Road. The journey took over seven hours and was reported in the local press.

Six

Chapels and Churches

Interior of Penistone Church. Alterations made in the 1970s moved the alter forward and the organ and choir stalls to the back.

Netherfield Chapel. Founded in the 1780s from an original gift of £25.

Netherfield Chapel. Extensions were made in the 1890s. The road at the Chapel side was lowered and the milestone reading 'London 177 miles' was incorporated into the boundary wall.

Spring Vale Primitive Methodist Chapel, *c.* 1920. The foundation stone for the chapel was laid on 3 October 1896. The small tower was later to topple during high winds. Those involved in painting the Chapel (green) are: Thomas Steele, Owen Roebuck and Cecil Penney.

Interior of the modern Spring Vale Chapel 1975. The pews are the only remnant of the old chapel.

A Sunday School group outside Thurlstone Primitive Methodist Chapel. On the outside of the building (now covered) was the inscription 'Beautiful Zion'.

Thurlstone and Millhouse
Methodist Chapel (previously
West End Chapel), *c.* 1930. The
chapel was built in 1915 and
received a new organ made by
H.J. Nelson of Durham in 1927.

Thurlstone St. Saviours Parish Church. The Church was only completed in 1906 thanks to a
donation of £6,000 by a Miss Bray.

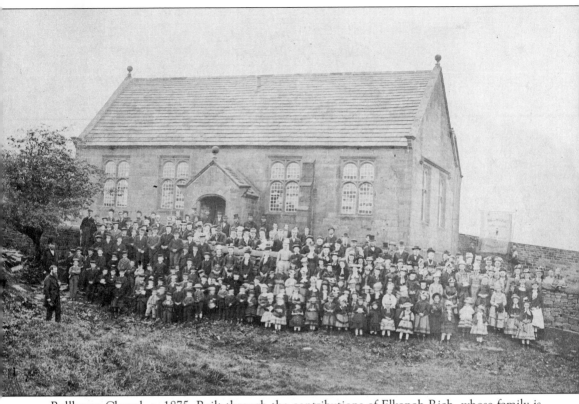

Bullhouse Chapel, c. 1875. Built through the contributions of Elkanah Rich, whose family is buried at the Chapel, in 1692. It is one of the oldest Non-Conformist Chapels in the country. This picture was taken for the Jubilee celebrations for the Sunday School.

The Reverand Joseph Bardsley, *c.* 1920. Bardsley was the Minister of Bullhouse Chapel for over 50 years (1869–1921). A plaque resides in the chapel to the Reverand and his daughter.

WESLEYAN CHAPEL INGBIRCHWORTH

Wesleyan Chapel, Ingbirchworth, *c.* 1920s.

Seven

Schooltime

Thurlstone Infants School, September 17 1907.

Penistone Girls, *c.* 1898.

Penistone Grammar School, *c.* 1890s. The School moved to Weirfield House in 1893.

A Grammar School Class of 1968. Those identified so far are: Paul Dyson, Richard Walker, Phillip Gill, Keith Dryden, Steven Godley, Steven Healey, Steven Dennison, Andrew Earnshaw, Micheal Dean, Julie Phallack, Andrew Haig, Steven Harley, Ann Forbes, Celia Fisher, Gillian Ford, Elizabeth Ellsworth, Bronwyn Corriss, Julie Fretwell, Bridget Doyle.

The old Grammar School site just before the move to Weirfield in 1893. The Grammar School is one of the oldest in England dating back to 1392.

Weirfield House Grammar School at the turn of the century. Fulford ('A' Block) was constructed by the side of these buildings in 1911.

Millhouse School, c. 1920s.

Millhouse School Concert

1912.

Chair to be taken at 7-15 p.m.

On Friday, January 19th, by

T. SMITH, Esq., of Turton House.

On Saturday, January 20th, by

J. HINCHLIFFE, Esq., J.P., of Wellcliffe.

Accompanist - - - Mrs. Eddy, Penistone.

PROCEEDS FOR ADDITION TO SCHOOL LIBRARY.

James H. Wood, The Don Press, Penistone

Millhouse School Concert, 12 January 1912.

126

At the back of the old Workhouse in Penistone.

A Sunday School outing in the 1920s.

The back of the Grammar School, *c.* 1930s. Ada Blacker was the cook at the Grammar School for many years.